AFTER JUBILEE

AFTER JUBILEE

BRIONNE JANAE

BOAAT
2017

Printed in the United States of America

Cover image by Ify Chiejina
Book design and cover design by Laura Theobald
Author photo by Amelia Golden

BOAAT Press is a publisher and builder of books.
ISBN: 978-0-9994922-0-8

BOAAT Press
520 7th Street NE
Charlottesville, VA 22902
www.boaatpress.com

V.

Postcard

always the dark body hewn asunder; always
  - Natasha Trethewey

always the dark body hewn asunder; always
the rope and the stretched neck broken, always shadows
streaked across ashen faces, nights darkness wrecked

with torchlight, always the body blacker than clay
mob below upright glaring, always lack stowed
in the hollowness between dark ribs. the spec-

tacle flash, framed and looking up. always some slack
nigger sorry, looking down. always the rending
the parted flesh, the body broken never blessed

always a sacred tree, and dead weight, the dark roots wracked
with guilt. forever and always, here, an ending
the fatal twitch ticking down till final breath.

always the flesh bared to scarcely masked desire.
always murder, stolen sex, helpless overcome with fire.

I.

Swing Dance, a Spiritual

tonight we grip our partners and swing,
one hip-flung moment of supplication
and release, baby hold me and baby let me twirl

our sweat silkened bodies linked—shoulders
to a gear pumping life into lonely flesh. we dance
on borrowed boards to borrowed tunes, wade

through water without the dogs and desperation,
we get down to the big band bopping beat.
we get the best of the world, if we can forget.

most nights you can. and it's daisies
on a graveless hillside, it's everything beneath your eyes
cradled in the soft palms of childhood.

except how to unremember the assaults
on your childhood—granny's hands cloaked in suds,
the skillet shaking beneath the faucet

and men is dogs and she telling you how
and you too young to stop her, know too much
too little to understand. *and he touched his hands all over me.*

and I wanted to scream, wanted to wake my father.
you can forget this most days. keep granny at the stove,
day before thanksgiving, nursing a pot a gumbo

and asking if you've been reading your bible.
but tonight this man asks you to dance, grabs
your wrist, yanks you about

like a hound still yet unbroken
and you know it then. this man is old—
old and white enough to stroke your granny

on a night ride through texas and get away with it.
you come into your blackness in the mirror of a whitewashed
dance studio—you are your grandmother

sitting between your father and the tow truck driver
in the dead of night, on a country road
you are eighteen only.

no matter how close you tuck into your father's side
you must touch them both, the outer side of your thigh
come to rest against the ragged jeans of the stranger,

the wide of your hips already filling the space
from one man to the next.

Flight

you're sitting in daddy's old
        ford explorer, before it got torched

by gang bangers.
        day's bright.

the sun's rays almost
        obscure the dull red of the traffic light

hanging at the end of the bridge
        over the dried up river that daddy says

is man made, and marks the border
        between the O.C. and L.A.

where daddy has caught
        your eye in the rearview.

you say, how come
        aint nothing but white people

live near Granny house
        and round about Mo and Pa

everybody black? he say, well,
        and stall like a man twice his age

on a porch swing
        at the edge of life

he say, used to be white folk
        lived in the cities. black folk

come from down south
        and moved in and even decent

white folk didn't like it.
          one day they rose up

and said its too many coloreds.
            they left for the burbs. and you know what?

soon enough, a few black folk
          with a couple dollars to their name

looked around, said it's too many
          niggers, and baby girl, they went and ran off too.

Abduction

in order to stretch your fear of men
and white vans momma tells you

they put twigs inside your private parts
says they hurt simply for the sake of it.

brain knotted, you sit on the old fuchsia carpet
calmed by the feel of the strands

between your fingers. you try to grasp the pleasure
in the act—because surely there must be

pleasure for these shapeless men
or else why bother with the ugliness

of hurt and snatching up girls in the first place.
this the closest you ever come to talking sex

with momma, and it's too soon then
to couple the trauma with the word

or even the secrets of your own body.
and besides you're still a long ways off

from the shame of girls sold down
to new orleans for comfort—how inevitable though

that it finds you, the horror, a phantom
at your neck, pressing, the unfamiliar weight

nestled between your breast. and yet, regardless
of how a kidnapped girl got ushered

into that world you learn to breathe again,
a shallow breath, and sometimes even forget.

Postcard: Billy Harrison Speaks

- for Laura Nelson 1878-1911

when they had done with her and the torches
were extinguished with dew, and she lay
like something decaying in mulch,
blood muddied hair, slip bunched about her hips.
when she smelled like the sheets at *Rising Sun*,

and men scattered like mice before lamplight
and her breath still came like a locomotive before it stalled,
and her arms were tucked beneath her
and her eyes swollen shut. when George had gone for the camera,
took to finding the perfect spot upriver and we were ready
to cast her down to swing beside her son.

I knelt and unbound her arms
to pull them still warm in the sleeve
to lift the brassiere to its proper place
button the blouse, fetch the skirt
from among thick roots where one man pissed
onto the bark. I slid her naked feet
through the opening, lifted the hips
fixed the clasps about her waist.

and we stood on the bridge as the *Canadian* stretched
calm beneath us, their bodies reflecting with the trees.

Aubade

- June 18, 2015

when only birds toll the hour
and barely a hint of our star tints the sky,

I stir breathless and warm,
too foggy to know the cause. asthma maybe,

anxiety my little incubus, or just an arm
resting at my neck. If ever this gasping were enough

to kill, I pray not to wake. death can't be so bad
without the presence of the dying.

fingers wrapped about my inhaler, I squeeze the trigger once,
twice. life's breath forced from the chilled rigid mouth

down into the canals of my throat.
how much easier to take a life than to call it back.

at sunrise I wake to 9 dead in an AME church.
were I a poet who spoke with the sun

I'd have only curses, why wake me,
why wake me for this.

Dan Henry

- for Papa

he sat on the porch like a man wanting a pipe.
elephant ears flapped in Santa Ana gales, warm

wanton with lushness. his eyes haunted and frail
could not see them. he rocked and rusted

then stilled, a man locked in his father's pose,
he saw again, Miss'sippi back woods creeping to the fields

God's sigh sifting the bare cotton bolls
and wondered if ole mister wouldn't yield

a fair price for the labor of his hands.
'cept now he owned this porch, never stressed

bout no mister but sat a beer bellied old man
enthroned, telling his grands bout his first nor-easter

how as a boy he worried the docks
with labor and escaped his father's pine box.

II. 1950s

- for my grandparents

Going North

eyes caked with morning grime you whisper, *good morning.*
                    is it time already?
our sheet walls flutter
like your lips against my ear, the wind
filling them with sweet nothings
about the factory job your gonna get, a house
up in St. Louis, and only a couple months later,
me in pearls cooking on a gas burning stove.

you wanna know if I can see it too
but I can't concentrate with Pa's snore
still filling the cabin.
                    it can't be time already
I haven't figured out what to do
when you are gone, and our walls
are just puddles wrinkling on the floor.

train ain't gone wait all day, you say, rising
like the top end of a biscuit coaxed by fire.
ma's gone say I should've cooked you a good breakfast,
before you go, but I can't lift a finger from rippling
round this swelling belly we wrought writhing behind the juke joint
that night Son House was hollering out them "Walking Blues."

and so, barefoot and threadbare I follow you outside, refusing
to study your shoulders tugging at the straps of your overalls,
the razor burn lining your jaw, or the grease whitening your hair.
        it's too late to try and remember you now.
no, I don't think I'll walk with you to the station.

at the edge of Pa's field, I pull you
between the corn stalks, my hand resting on your neck,
more like prayer than affection. you kiss me,
coal black lips stilling my own before I can warn you
to stay clear of tree branches or men

with rifles and rope. eyes alive and earnest
you promise to come back.
my hand stays on your neck till you walk on
the corn stalks trembling as you go.

Sharecropper

the morning her water broke her father got up early, trudged
to the field, took up the plow, left the stove top churning water boiling
over. he didn't stop to stay the fire. all morning he worked
on an empty stomach. he had no place there. he pushed the plow
down deep into the earth, till his shirt clung to him like a man going under.

~

when his daughter was coming
the women folk put him out
he shuffled only as far as the porch,
sat on the swing teetering
legs digging into the floor boards,
the swing rising, rusted hinges croaking
then the release, the drop forward then back.

his pa visited. found him jittering like a clown.
without anyone to offer them lemonade
they chewed tobacco, spit curds all over,
till the air grew sour and their jaws ached.
Pa left and he tossed a pale of water over the porch,
watched it dry, and teetered for hours with nothing
but his wife's screams for company.
then she grew quiet a long while
                              and his daughter came.

~

she too young and I hates that wanna be city slick boy.
his overalls always too clean, and lord knows he aint coming back for her.
shoulda shot him dead first time he set foot on my land,
talking bout Hattie's pregnant and we gone get married soon as he got money.
and damned if the girl wasn't smiling like a fool. and now
now listen to her, hollering like her ma, and what can I do? if it comes to it,
they not cutting out that baby. I won't allow it.
child aint worth a damn to me without my little gal.

Church Song

*"The most prestigious black churches... attracted some newcomers from
the South, but their formal, high-toned services discomforted others"*
-Ira Berlin, *The Making of African America*

like house niggas plating yams at they white folks table
demons tucked away deep in they britches,
rigid as the gears of a delta bound steamer
they took to their Boston pews, good books in hand
noses to heaven like they's tryna lodge a whiff
of God's sweat up each nostril

and at the altar this woman
singing with so much soul she had Jesus
stripped in the stained glass beside her
gut drawn, breath coming fast,
his colored sun moving light against her skin

she had blues in her moaning
tears leaking all Friday night's sin
how the whole church didn't groan with her
is proof they never seen God
or really longed for a woman
like a deer wanting water

so my soul thirsts for her
her in that daisy'd cotton dress
with room at the knee for a hand up the hem
her with those holy eyes wet
and weeping, her lifted for me like I was god
and she my body made for worship

                    at the end of service
the women folk's fans were hornet wings beating the air
and they eyes slung muck like buck shot
but it didn't make no nevermind
she moved through them all like clear water
cutting 'round jagged rock

Sisters

- for Momo

one of those days water calls to the young
pulls them by their toes to banks

where the river slows and the sun
dives below and the bed

rises to meet their clumsy feet
to let them pass gently splash

and drag each other under.
malleable as mud my sister

was always willing to give.
to be shoved down so I could thrust

my head above the water like a gator
snapping at a passing gull.

we spent the day baking
raisins turning—dark wrinkled things—

I insisted on casting a line at sunset
though she begged to go home

before daddy had time to worry
and slide his belt from the loops.

we got what she feared. daddy lashing
culling welts like a cross roads preacher

gathers souls. I always ran
twisted swung back but she just stood

crying. after when daddy had settled
down to eat our fish and I sat pushing

heads round my plate she said start with the eyes
and be careful of biting the skull.

Mechanic

this man leaning over the car's open hood all dust
and sweat shine, eying with such softness

the sun heated metal, wires crawling round like children
in water, something between play

and pecking order, this man caked to the wrist
with dirty black oil, who likes wupping

niggers just to watch 'em jump
and drag, as a child I could not imagine

this man a boy with my daddy.
could not see on his face daddy's brief nose

and eyebrow-less eyes sunk in
looking like they wanted to give up

the world. folks say this man's father
was all piss, fists, and moonshine—

praise the earth veiled skin that kept my daddy
fatherless. I could not imagine what this man wanted

with my small dark self but my father said mr. thomas
is going to make me, daddy's first born,

a mechanic, says they haven't seen each other
since they were my age, says to mind my yessirs.

mr. thomas-yessir asks if I want to know
how to make her pop and shout, his eyes

like we are not just meeting. he puts a hand
on my shoulder pushing me closer

to the wires, and I could see how they had hoped
to be entangled, how they were formed,
each of them to be held apart.

Holy Thursday

before going north my pa took us down
to the river. John in the Jordan, he waded
waist deep in mucky water, swept his palms up
and sang out, come on baby swim to me.

I remember how momma turned away
smoothed the edges of her apron to busy
that tremble in her finger tips. how I leapt in
and went under, my pa hauling me like hay—

then a chill on my wet skin.
I cried in his arms awhile, but he stooped,
and the water passed gently
and he bounced me on his hip like a babe

till I stilled, and lay back with just his calloused
hand beneath me—floating

*

first time he left momma shaking on the steps
of her folks house, he was just a boy war bound
and eager for his hold on the world. he came home
with more to tell than any set of ears could hear.

heading to church on Sundays he liked to recall
the height of all those grim grey churches and wonder
how a man ever got high enough to lay the bricks.
mostly he loved the pictures in glass—his favorite,

christ kneeling before the disciples, a frail foot
cupped in his hands as if to kiss it. that day
as I dried in the spring sun, pa knelt in the riverbed.
sighing he bared momma's foot in the water, kneaded

the dirt free from her sole, and she steadied her fingers
in his hair, eyes fixed, begging, come back.

Yellow Girl

when they spit him coal black burning
like smoke from a northern steeple
and he breathed need

of my arms. when he came back broken
wanting to have me kneeling
dragging my lips

over every inch of flesh to rework life piecemeal.
when he found you yellow sucking at my breast
pale as cornbread batter livid in cast iron.

when you were unmarked
and he looked but couldn't see his hold
when he refused to be your father

and I gave up striking flint but didn't forget
the way his hand sank down my belly.
when I let him whisper rape

whisper white man's baby whisper how they just take
and take and take. when he held me and silence
was an apron stuffed in my mouth

when it was stitched with my mother's shame.
when I was a girl again learning not to ask
about my daddy or wonder

why my hair got so gold when summer burned.
when I loved you but wanted to clean
this dirty blood. when I left you

in the sun and you screamed. when you lay red
and peeling. when your father's courage
came with corn liquor season and the rifle rang.

when I begged him to run. when he ran.
when he was just a small thing moving in blackness.

West

- for Granny

he let himself be choked by dust
my father bent over the roads edge hocking
up phlegm like it would kill him.

was always the same *boy where the hell*
you think you going nigger whose car
you done stole now

seemed like he'd been shook down
every town our old coach hiccupped through
since we left momma waving in the corn

my sister clawing for the breast beneath
that thin stained apron. she'd lost two children to hunger
and we left to give this last one a chance.

it'd been days of trouble and I had learned
to mind my shoes as he answered the men
from that broken angle. body bowed

hand clutching at the hood
eyebrows and neck racked up. he had his story
let them pull themselves above him

as he crooned how he was just a poor old reverend
chasing his ungrateful flock who the Lord somehow loved
and so called him to drag them one by one back

to His good ole south. he peddled that story
from louisianna to california and I wanted to ask
if he was tired of bending

of being the dirt those men trod more firmly
into the ground. I stayed silent. it was not a thing to be spoken of
and besides I knew my father.

III. DONOR

- for Edward "Juju" Sutton 2010-2014

Corneas

in that moment he is still
taste of skin salt. lips pulling on middle fingers
a forgotten memory of the nipple in his mouth. *miraculous.*
he is. filled with impermanent teeth and laughter and screaming

and vital things. he is. and so the sun yields
to his body. *miraculous.* just look how his shadow, drawn
longer than he'll ever be, can dim the room just so.
and still his lungs pull the air. his hands
press into the window's screen. *miraculous.* he is.

the way it ripples around his fingers
without giving before its time. the way he yells puppy
cause it didn't exist before his eyes caught hold.
miraculous the way he is pure delight.

in that moment. the way he is,
then is not he. but vanished thing. *miraculous.* he is
what was. sound of a three year old opening on pavement.

*

I heard if a person jumps from a skyscraper
it's not the fall that kills them but the fear of impact.
what mercy. oh hush heart. what *miraculous* God
to still the life's breath before the break.

but he was so young. and what could he know of being broken.
in only three stories how could his heart learn peace.

recovered: Edward's corneas his gift may restore sight.
        the gift of restored vision is miraculous.

miraculous. that you, God, would take his life. violently.
        to be *miraculous.* to give sight.

Left Kidney

you the picture of what grandma calls
that *well with my soul* kind of faith, you fat
with foreign blood and so small, passed
from the body of a boy to the body of an old woman,

better half of your life elided in a breath
with such ease of acceptance, willingness to slough
off one self for the next, to assimilate into the viscera
of another without pulling at the sutures

or baiting the blood to conflict. how to name
the difference between you, who are without breath,
and I, without naming it bitterness. it must be said—
I envy you, living with no God imposed on the disorder

and no sense of order or what was broken and no one
to curse in prayer, and nothing worth praying to.

Liver

- for Edward and Vanessa Sutton

having borne all the way to the core of the earth
through darkness, passed the bones of the boy that was son
call him God's child now

what selfish God. having burned
on molten pitch, beheld the billowing light of hell
and burrowed still

having opened against the rock
felt fresh that cleaving separation of the body
from the body. having muddied the ground with your blood

and thought maybe he could be made flesh
anew, having called for *ruach*
and learned there is no life begun down here.

having opened your flesh
oh release me from the flesh
having given up on death

and heard tell of a mouth to this low place
an opening into something other than flesh
having dreamed you walked into the light

your scars grimacing at the sun
having hoped just a little, having given up on life,
come now, and remember, blooming

Heart

good friday Mo puts something in the ground
swiss chard or green beans.
a decade past she knelt to twist the soil
behind a succulent cactus, its spines
overgrown and sharp as syringes.
in the shadows she nestled a peach pit.
the first fruit ripened and she split the meat
between us. it was the sweetest thing.
once I culled a purple lily from the dead
Juju had just fallen, and I crooned my prayers
to the single living stalk till others sprang
from the dirt to hear my worry.
not one bud ever swelled to open.
Juju still lies dormant on a hillside.

*

here in what must be called God's periphery,
his hand grasping

for the baby needed only in fraction.
here where death is fulcrum

and this boy is formed to grow that boy
a purposed beating heart

and die. how not to wonder, here,
at the choosing of the mother.

her body halved between the warm
and the still. how behold the man,

silly enough to sow hope
in a namesake, without breaking.

sometimes there's nothing left
but to bless the child, the live one

with a stolen heart humming in his chest.
oh be blessed boy be blessed.

Picture After the Big Game

it is october in california,
five months after their brother's fall.

in Jeremiah's arms they smile
and he is no longer mine

standing beneath the friday night lights
but a giant. his body, bulked

out with football pads, invincible.
you can see it in the way they clutch

at him, my baby brother,
as if it would make him theirs, Juju

come up from the grave
to hold them for a moment.

how not to see the need of it on their faces
they the etymology of want:

absence of that vital thing. yet look
how they pose with the ease of children

from Gap retail magazines who have never
known hurt. even my brother

who likes to pretend he's too hard for joy
has exposed his teeth. Christ, teach me

to see them without the small boy chilled
beneath the veil. teach me to find Juju

living in Kayleigh's out swung hip,
Michael's cheeks, Karry's brow. Christ

teach me to look and see all you have given
and not all there is still left to take.

IV. SLOCUM, TEXAS
1910

After Jubilee

spread the bolls to shuck their down
still sow-thistle flowering and necks to bear the yoke.

still the north star tilting north,
a need to cull the freed to freedom.

the weary still cover their dead with groans
and You slumber

deaf to the faithful calling. Lord hear us
witness our yearning,

bodies grown ancient, thin as that old shanty woman,
knee bones pushing through her skirt.

yet look how she leans forward, still turning
at the sun, still expectant. God

we have been a long time waiting, give up Your bed,
Lord, walk with us.

Cutting

again the blessed sunday bird went to fire whole.
your momma, all shined in her church things turned over

the shanty, she hunting for that good butcher
knife all day, cursing daddy and begging *Christ ha'mercy.*

you can hear her from the maize, you kneeling, knees dug
in the earth like this the last time, for sure, this the last

time. you don't know no more how long
you called yourself quitting but still can't forget

those little hurts. like how the veins jump
from momma's throat when she whip eggs whites for easter pudding,

haul an ax over her back, or strike daddy with leaden fists
when he stagger home late slathered in blues.

and so early before the friday night hootch fled
his body you filched daddy's butcher knife

hid in the tall swaying stalks settling your want in blood
crawling from your skin a freed thing calling on God.

Weaning

you remember the brown of your momma's nipples
puckered and sliding from this new brother's lips
how she ran her finger round
teasing the idle bud to attention.
to you it seemed to pout, resist
the fingers corralling its small dark self toward pasture.
you fill a tattered sack with dirt
draw eyes and mouth with mud and press
against the flatness of that old flowered dress
where your tits hid soft and inattentive.
called it baby, bounced it when it cried
smothered its hunger with warmth. once
before this brother came you snuck
into some white folks barn to stroke
the udder of the heifer with teats so large
they parted the grass where she walked.
you wanted to put your tongue on the soft pink flesh
just as you wanted your momma's nipple
in your mouth, to suck, and pull
like you pulled fiz up the straw
that day daddy brought you to town for a treat.
too soon your momma washed your sack doll
and taught you how to fill it with sugared water
tie the ends just so, place the rough corner
in the baby's mouth and squeeze.
that night gripped by what your brother had lost
you hardly notice daddy across the room spreading
your momma with his thighs, back bent
head rutted in her breast, biting.

Blues Poem: Good Looking Woman

Well, rocks 'n gravel make a solid road, sugar
It takes a good-lookin' woman to make a good-lookin' whore

y'cant tell me you aint missin my early morning jam, mixed in grits
'member how you took your breakfast sticky, jam swirlin in your grits
aint but a few quarters babe, sit down, have your plate fixed

you eat cantaloupe like a po' boy, suckin flesh from the rind
you put down cantaloupe like you starvin, lips buried in the rind
lord knows you Mississippi po' boys love good melon off the vine

I only made cobbler with peaches layed up under my door
I make cobbler cause peaches always ripenin up under my door
Babe how you gone get mad bout a little extra juice spilt on the floor

careful with that sugar cane, it'll snap in your rough hands
gentle with me suga babe, I'aint what's strippin your cracked hands
go'on toss me at the wall then, but I'aint never lied down like no lamb

Babe you was like biscuits in a firewood stove, hot too quick and burnin
like biscuits in some young girls stove, you was always black and burnin
hear you done rode in Sheriffs new car, don't look like you'll be returnin

Breaking Man

you ever seen a man
break a mare between his legs
wild one, kind bucks
just at the stench
of a man, back buckled
haunches twitching like jelly roll
legs splayed

he'd run her ragged
round the bull pen
no rest or water, just
her shoulder cracking the curved wood
whip's snap chasing behind her
naked hooves kicking up dust
a dry scream drug up from her throat

this after he'd forced
the bridle between her teeth
her knees in the dirt, body
arched like a hissing cat
no, no more of this
you'll never find a man less gentle

and after he'd driven the spirit
from her bones
he'd rein her closer
closer with each trip round
till she could only still
then he'd lay his hands on her
panting, and speak softly

once I loved a man
like a mare does the breaking hand
kind liked to clap yellow gals cross the face
just to watch they skin turn

and I took him between my legs
thinking to make him mine
till he left me broken and ragged
stripped of the call to run free

God I've Grown

a woman afraid of small things:
the outhouse black when the moon

is thin and hunched behind clouds
gray like spirits gathered overhead

the bend of saplings when winds rush
and rivers rise, of going under—

of higher ground. of momma
drinking hootch and striking flint,

of kindling, of kitchen fire, of glowing ash,
pa's sunday suit and church folk whispering

him pulling a switch and raising
my dress, of blood between my legs

going dry, it turning brown
it disappearing, of this tiny body

that lies so still—lord I can't raise this boy
with his daddy up north

or dead in a ditch or cozied up
with some high chinned gal

with pearls round her neck lord
be with me, lord be with me.

Preserves

it stained the dirt like blood stretching
after too long cooped up in the body
everywhere the jar in pieces slender sharp.

I had bout as much business in missus' jams
as James under my skirt. when he stopped calling
his need cool as a pie fly ridden on the sill

and I had gone weeks without enough—
enough fever in my skin, fullness in my belly,
drumming in my chest. I went there

with want. plunged my tongue
in the honeyed fruit, nursed on sweetness
blackberries from summer when he lay me

among brambles and burrs. his momma
further along hollering for the basket
upended at our feet. at first it was his need

but then it was mine. and it was easy to get lost
with his eyes burning like that bible bush at the sight of me
stooped, scrubbing his floor. and it was hard

never getting to say when, when hands yanked
at my hair pulled on my breast, when they gentled
when I could have my fill or go without.

hidden in the shed I flung that jar down
cause it wasn't enough. my arm arched with power
got lugging wet linens to the line. it shattered

and I knelt there in the dust my skirt raised like the sun
after a night spent waiting. I can't say what took me
to that edge, to that slender shard of glass,

what drew it hard across my thigh and left blood.
God forgive me, but it felt right to have done something.
to have a wound somewhere hidden my hands had opened.

Maple Jar

to the knuckles my fingers
dipping in. mouth. the need
to get this bitter from my tongue
bury it in sweetness. even as a girl
I could taste momma's ache like soot
in the air. how I remember fear.

how she could holler my name
like it wasn't hers. like it was pus
filled in her cheek and bursting open
like something daddy'd found
at the crown of some gal's blues slung legs.
I never tarried long then.
to find her sitting on the back porch
thighs spread west, taking the sun
like it wouldn't shine no more tomorrow.

dust. my feet covered in it. standing there.
smiling. as if seeing me could please her.
no. nothing.

just that hacking cough and pinning
me between her knees, to pull loose
my hair, yank week old naps
from dirty edges, and arc her fingers
to scratch the dandruffs free from my skull.
all around me hair would fall.

then kneeling before the pail,
fear of never being clean,
of water, of soap forced to lather.

but by the fire side
she'd put on a mother's hands
and sing a song she thinks her momma sang once.

and lay my head, wet in her lap, and braid
tight my clean hair, now and then stopping
to stroke my small face, or lean down
and kiss me softly on the brow.

Deliverance

aunt janie I saw undone by the stove
something bout loading the hacked wood into fire,
bout how her boy used to grind out muddy blues
for girls pale as sharecropped cotton
bout the first time, the last time she heard tell he stole away,
had been stowed away in the earth
had her gnawing her fingernails down to bloody stubs.

something bout knowing it could happen
and I could be bent collecting myself
from the ground like momma, wild
beating the horse from the crumpled thing that was my sister.
seen enough of women weeping over what they
drove pulsing from their bellies, things one day laughing
one day cut down from the sky.

I know nothing keeps the bones where they ought be
but my arms wrapped round this body
and so woman cannot be naturally a holder of things
if she must hold herself too, and I am too much need. at the altar

plumed and shining preacher's wife and Mothers' Board wrestle
to wrench my arms away say *send the spirit bellowing*
from your gut girl raise them hands go'on get delivered.
how to say I been delivered by the hoodoo woman
my baby, blood song at my thigh.

Momma Blues

they say aint a woman living could hold a son for too long

my boys daddy could make a guitar croon
so your small clothes fell like apricot drippings for a cobbler
had lips like water
hands steady with dry spell blues

I was big with my boy when we cut down my sometime man
sang home his chariot
stayed up all night with his momma to mourn

I kept after my boy with a quick swishing switch
scoured his ears let him flail in the river
the name of the father the son

still his daddy in him stretched his shoulders out long
and he always had cause to pluck and groan

snared a man's full bellied call in the chords of his throat
his feet so soft they itched to roam and a boy is not a peach
he can't be canned he can't be saved

and it gets hard these mornings after to pull on my stockings
to see which boy whose boy been caught up

Queen of Night

when I could only watch Bo clutching our dark squirming love,
hymn song frantic on his lips. and the hoodoo woman still worked
below packing me with poultice and fresh cloth and night still hung
around us black as blessing. I asked to see the pale of what came after
the birth, blood curdled with excess, and I thought,
if only all was like this and the sun never shone
tomorrow, never flayed her with light in a world where darkness
like hers condenses hate easy as droplets on a glass of sweet tea.

before she left, the hoodoo woman paused, maybe feeling something like mercy,
she lifted her body turned to Bo and said there is no god
will look kindly on that girl, but I will bury this blood in your flower bed
and where it lies will come up tulips dark as a ballad to blue black skin
and as she grows bind them into a garland and crown her beloved,
queen of night, and pray the earth spring forth to protect her.

Love Spell

thread at the sleeve of your everyday dress
spry thing to be pulled like a pigs tail
and released. a bitch at your feet

I'd wrap the thread round my fingers
like drawing in an empty fishing line.
as if I could catch you. with daddy gone

you'd put the good chair in the doorway
and sit, arms like vines hanging for hours.
your eyes, spirits combing the woods

keen on something to possess.
when the thread broke, the chair's legs
dug further into the mulch, and your hair

was moss at your neck. afraid to lose you,
I tried passing time with the raised edge
of your slipper, tracing dew lines bleeding

through the fabric, but you were too often
barefoot. momma I would have loved to drag
my finger along the veins of your foot

to make them jump beneath your skin
to touch you, to turn your eyes on me. momma
is this how you love or is this how you love him

momma if I had gone into the woods would you
cast your spirits for me too, and be the trees
and the earth and the moss carrying me home.

Gut Bucket Blues

so you tired of my gut bucket blues,
　　　　thought you'd dust your broom and go
you too damn good for my gut bucket blues,
　　　　go'on pack your bags and go
we was the b.d. women of murdian city,
　　　　but guess now I aint shit no more

I hear the juke joints in chicago
　　　　got women jiving all night long
they say the blues men in chicago
　　　　got colored girls rocking all night long
you always been an easy rider babe,
　　　　sure you up their fucking through the dawn

we used to roll biscuits in the morning,
　　　　eat jelly rolls at noon nice and slow
we rolled biscuits in the morning,
　　　　damned if you didn't stroke your jelly nice and slow
now you cooking in some back door woman's kitchen,
　　　　with your apron slung down low

said you was a tumble weed baby,
　　　　aint got no roots to hold you down
swore you's a tumble weed sugar,
　　　　can't no roots ever hold you down
who's that yellow heffa at the crossroads,
　　　　the hell she got that keep you around

Resting Place

at the end uncle lay on the porch swing
too weak to make the old thing creak and low
with eyes fixed on that old hollowed tree
the march to fort sully roaming his mind
he told the story again
as if the rest of his life were lost
in the sameness of them kansas plains

we was men then
and the only way a man
gets a thing is with force
I'd been pinned my whole life
but it was my turn now
to shove a knee in some bodies chest
to let blood and come out living
I aint have a thing gainst them Indians
it was just my time

he'd always catch hold of me then
lock eyes or grab at my wrist
watching for me to pull away from his guilt
he put up this house because of that old tree
because it'd followed him here
from some stream cutting its way down a hill

except that kansas tree had been filled
with dirt and some dead *comanche*
maybe it kept him near his gods
my uncle only dreamed of being a man again,
of standing upright, tall in death
he always ended with the same plea
when I die don't bury me underground
like some common thing let me rest standing in my tree.

Cabin Child

we slept arms touching feet touching the crown
of a tangled head. we hacked on dust took air
damp with grime from a shack too drafty
for livestock. we were often waking

afraid as children are of even the smallest nighttime shudder.
Jacob called out most but who would answer?
imagine the old cripple who slumped lower and lower into the earth
really loved us. imagine my mother dead but still floating down

to lie with me in the lull of those quiet hours. imagine my father
free and a sailor working for a little something to give his baby.
yes. dream them anywhere but there. a stone's throw away
bone tired benumbed by slaving. each day it gets harder

to imagine my father as more than a stud pumping
into a choice mare. imagine he has not forgotten my name.

Newly Wed

in this one room shanty without windows
only one good sack of millet for hunger

and no matches I have risen from the bed
which is only a stolen sheet cast over straw

to cook you breakfast. I want to be good
for you. but what do I know of striking flint

or bringing anything to flames.
once my aunt tried to teach me

said lean in whisper your sins to smoke
said you could be forgiven by fire.

but momma lifted her nose at low labor
and I never learned how to burn my secrets.

we are not speaking now. momma and I.
she has her feelings about this dirt floor shanty

with no books and that flea hop bed
where you named me woman.

I know I won't be young forever but want forever
and I have seen how breast can fall in my family

but if I could cook you this millet
watch you eat and smile…damn it.

this flint wont spark. you startle awake
to me beating the dark rocks together

your eyes already keening
for something I don't yet know to call hunger.

I say teach me to light a fire
you say woman come back to bed.

At The Crossroads

- after Son House's "Dry Spell Blues"

the devil and that guitar writhe and fall
        dredging up squall heavy dry spell blues

kind rocks a man to the bone
        sends him home sweating hootch

crooning bout walking shoes
        and how pork chops is forty five cents a pound

and corn's only ten
        and soon he won't keep no woman

be chasing Berta down the western byroad
        and wouldn't you rather pick oranges 'stead of shucking maize.

        how to be woman enough to strip the roam from a man
keep him cupped in your palms barefoot

        and after good loving. should I stop his ears with corn husk
stuff his mouth with jelly roll

        fork my tongue set his skin ablaze
his hands busy in this overflowing flesh

        let them snake round and round these good hips.
no. momma says you got to haul the cast iron

        over your head rush wild swinging for glory
you got to beat the devil from the crossroads

        and keep what's yours at home.

Cotton Root

navel, tips of her toes,
from the nose to her eye's center,
palms soft as good soil, I kiss her
everywhere and she is discovery,
is each new piece of herself. to think
my sister who fed me mud cakes
made this fulsome tiny thing
and with such an ugly man. you just know
my baby would've been beautiful.

*

before my first year at Oberlin we planted azaleas.
with daddy's good rake I taught momma
how to comb the rocky earth, part its tresses
raise its shifts, lay the seeds in bed to rest.
gently I covered it all in manure.
momma watched me toiling, clucked at my dirty hands
called this slave labor
what granddad worked hard to forget
and wouldn't it be a shame for him to see you
carrying on like this in the muck.
with blood kin daddy says there's times to bite down
remember who kept you here
breathing on God's green earth
like granddad's momma, how she scraped
the dogwood tree, brewed the bark
pulled her son back to life again and again
even when folks said he wasn't made to survive.
daddy says *all of us owes our lives to momma*

*

sooner or later every god wants blood
life for life, pain for smooth unrended flesh

forgive me you still unborn thing
first of my angels forgive me
there are ways of parting
and times to give in to yourself
I climbed on your daddy that day
with the chickens squawking in the corn
and the mules gawking
cause he couldn't come with me
and I wasn't asking him to wait
and now its dawn
and two weeks late
and God must be appeased
and I can't go on living with you
and its time to boil the cotton root
and sit and drink and wait for deliverance

First Rites

keen on mining that train breaking cry
from his sisters wide craw, he knelt

driving Elena's doll through mud,
a planter's prince without the stink

of toil in mud. I watched him
from the other side of the line,

linens and his pa's small things between us
catching the damp july air as it passed

nothing would be dry till tomorrow,
if then, and I hated the boy so close

to cleaned things. he bellowed to the neighbor kids
and I didn't say a damned thing to stop him.

the boys came, crouched beside him, flung filth
between them like a farrow without the sow's tits

to satisfy. an older boy muscled a sculpted
arm from the doll's mud blackened corpse,

and I could see the wild writhing in their bones.
where the rope came from, I don't know,

or who shouted first, *hoist the picaninny higher*
but I remember they laughed, all of them

their fathers' sons, and I wanted to strike
and feared them, as if even then

they were hunters of men, unabashed,
taking pleasure in what they had yet to learn

is best done in darkness.

Rent

- Marsh's General Store July 29, 1910

when sweat reeks of kerosene
and dust sandpapers the throat
day when the river is a long ways off
and you want what's owed
and what's owed cannot be rendered
cannot be given wholly of one person
and besides this person has bared his teeth.

on the porch idle hands fell so silent
there was nothing left to hear
but the heat settling like an unshorn sheep.
even Miss Molly whose mouth
flapped as freely as a fan on easter sunday
was silent, leaning against the walls.

I could tell from how Marsh fixed
on the windowsill with the sun
hitting him full in the face
that today was not a day for Mr. Alford.

I tried everything to ease the way
Alford's eyes was cutting at Marsh.
I praised the height of this years cotton
swore up and down his was the tallest
waived cobbler and sweet corn
under his nose and fluttered my lashes
and swished my skirts. I told him how business
was so slow and those deadbeats outside
wouldn't buy a thing. I promised him his money.

but Marsh never liked a show,
his eyes popped up from the sill
and locked on Alford like a bull tired of the pen.
he say I don't owe this peckerwood nothing,

spit at his feet. must a been the right breeze
or the crowd of negros outside the door,
but Alford didn't say a thing.
he just walked out the store boiling, red.

And Then

- July 29, 1910

now they are more than just sparks in the trees,
booming pockets of sound breaking the dusk
you see them advancing. the brown of their boots
parting the grass, the hootch shimmying, the unstopped
bottle, their shoulders, the rifles like sticks in boys' hands cocked
for play. you know from how the rope hangs, the not yet noose,
that this is fun, and they must surely find you. even the musk
from your body is belabored with this truth. like disease

it moves your skin, an impatient fear, eager to have it over.
hidden at the window you think of Bo running from their fever
think Bo and wish him here, and far from here, Bo your keeper

Bo and when you first turned round and round
his shanty like a pony itching for a way
free of the corral. you think how your shift clung
to your thighs all damp somewhere between
flight and crooning for nakedness, to be seen
to be loosed from this flush of skin and tongue
and flesh. then just before his fingers convince you to splay
your body, before they touch the down

between your legs, then. you wish it were then now, and Bo
swaggering home with the smell of blues, Bo curling your toes
and not this fear, not your body bowing, ready for the cracking blow.

Telephone Wires

- July 29th 1910

you don't see them dancing in what is almost a breeze
sifting the thick july night. lifeless,
dangling from the wooden pole, seen easy as a girl child
just beneath the surface all fat with water.
if you really looked you'd see them, but what would be gained.

already the town is silent, twitching its ears like a buck
wary of the hunter. the saloon, closed. Marsh's general store
with its stock of rifles, barricaded. as if the fire arms
would come out gunning for the innocent. even the road
is spooked, the dust refusing to rise as we walk.

you been changed, since they said yes at Oberlin.
your lips stretched with high words like *insufferable,*
liberation, ignorance. I remember when we spent the day
sun drunk sprawled at the river's edge and I culled blues
from your cunt and your head fell back like you wanted
to call on God but couldn't fix on how to get your jaw gears rolling again.

and after, when you found the braid of knotty brown hair,
ribboned and lapping at the river's edge
like a weed loosed from the muddy bottom,
I saved you for the first time. you stood struggling to cleave your tongue
from the roof of your mouth. to force out the word. drowned.
I lied. pointed to the even shorn end of the braid. a girl,
yes, but still alive like a dog shucking its heavy pelts for summer.

what went down your thigh that dawn
after months spent fucking is no secret.
your skin on my tongue like grits in the morning

now runs with caster oil.
to taste the change on you like the river turned
after passing through the girl,
her fingernails, her small parts, her teeth.
how to taste her, like the baby
still lingering at your lips—without weeping—

on your knees
beneath you right eye,
drooping as if you too are leaving,
at your hair line
so much blood.

they shot my brother—if it were only so simple
now—*they shot my brother*—you're stuck
on calling for help—*they shot my*
brother—and how can I tell you—*they shot*
my brother—they shooting all our brothers
they shot—and there won't be no calling
on anyone—*they shot*—but God
—*they*—they cut the phone wires—*they shot my*—
don't you see them hanging from the poles.

spirits in the trees
hush love hush love
go'on fly home

must we call the snatches of light
rifles seeking flesh, or could they simply be lightning
bugs signing there love through blackness.
come. don't stare down the road too long
or notice how quickly it submits to the forest
come love, we must not stay here

beneath the street light. we'd best not
walk too far into darkness.

V.

In Defense of Violent Protest or To Those Who Would Shame Them for Rioting or A Poem for Black Mothers

because we always too dark for sight
we must speak with the tongue of the sightless
release bricks like tears loose
toxins from blood,
shroud our shoulders in black smoke
shawl against winds of neglect,
beloved come, illuminate the night

cause we one body and if you carve
out my right side, leave it pooling on pavement
hours exposed no death rights no grace
shouldn't I scream, please,
help me understand, do you think me monster
some fleshless phantom that can bear
the sight of my body staining
the street and not cry out

hear me, we not built for silence

because now aint the time to talk
to God, body teach this phantom spirit to cast
off submission, shuck this yearning
for peace, shout spirit be still
till can't be no more still—
then, body remember me those old
testament ways of heat and blazing pyres
and let God look down at a creation on fire

and if this is what it must be
this, just one pass of the grindstone,
a single step in the erosion of my body into ash
then consider this our ritual

sacrament, holy, preparation for the embalming
of our own children, the ones we will bring screaming
into life, in spite of fear
and grip to our bodies like death
till they be black death embodied
cold on the boiling asphalt
and wont we be ready then
—yes—wont we be ready

Notes

The epigraph to "Blues Poem: Good Looking Woman" was taken from the song "Early in the Mornin" sung by the 22, Hard Hair, Little Red, and Tangle Eye. The song was recorded on Parchman Farm 1947-1948 by Alan Lomax.

In "Gut Bucket Blues" the phrase "b.d. women" is short for "bull dagger" or bully "dyke women," and was a colloquial term for "lesbian" during the early 1900s.

"Resting Place" was inspired by the diaries of J. Danly Budd (MS Am 1878.1), which can be found at the Houghton Library, Harvard University. In the diary Budd reports resting near a tree where a Native American man was buried.

"Rent," "And Then," and "Telephone Wires" were written after reading about the massacre that took place in Slocum, Texas in 1910. Only eight bodies were found after the attack; however, the local sheriff reported that he believed many more died whose bodies would never be found. The incident was reported in many newspapers around the country when it happened, but has yet to be written about in any major historical text.

Acknowledgements

Apogee Journal: "Left Kidney"

Bayou Magazine: "Swing Dance, A Spiritual"

Boaat: "Heart"

Breakwater Review: "Sisters," "Maple Jar"

Carve Magazine: "Going North"

Cincinnati Review: "At the Crossroads"

Fjords Review: "Mechanic"

Foundry: "Newyly Weds"

Hobart: "Queen of Night," "Church Song," "Cabin Child," "Telephone Wires"

jubilat: "In Defense of Violent Protest"

Kinfolks Quarterly: "After Jubilee"

Mobius: "Abduction"

Nashville Review: "Cutting"

New South: "Love Spell"

Plume: "Postcard: Billy Harrison Speaks"

Redivider: "Preserves"

Southern Humanities Review: "First Rites"

The American Poetry Review: "Corneas," "Liver," "Picture After the Big Game," "And Then"

The Comstock Review: "Momma Blues"

The Merrimack Review: "God I've Grown"

The Shallow Ends: "Breaking Man"

Toe Good Poetry: "Billy Harrison Speaks"

Twelfth House: "Yellow Girl," "Need"

Waxwing: "Aubade"

 **_Brionne Janae_** is a California native, poet and teaching artist living in Brooklyn. She is the recipient of the 2016 St. Botoloph Emering Artist award, a Hedgebrook and Vermont Studio Center Alumni and proud Cave Canem Fellow. Her poetry and prose have been published in *The American Poetry Review*, *Rattle*, *Bitch Magazine*, *The Cincinnati Review*, *jubilat*, *Sixth Finch*, *Plume*, *Bayou Magazine*, *The Nashville Review*, and *Waxwing* among others.